YOUR KNOWLEDGE HAS VALUE

- We will publish your bachelor's and master's thesis, essays and papers

- Your own eBook and book - sold worldwide in all relevant shops

- Earn money with each sale

Upload your text at www.GRIN.com
and publish for free

Bibliographic information published by the German National Library:

The German National Library lists this publication in the National Bibliography; detailed bibliographic data are available on the Internet at http://dnb.dnb.de .

This book is copyright material and must not be copied, reproduced, transferred, distributed, leased, licensed or publicly performed or used in any way except as specifically permitted in writing by the publishers, as allowed under the terms and conditions under which it was purchased or as strictly permitted by applicable copyright law. Any unauthorized distribution or use of this text may be a direct infringement of the author s and publisher s rights and those responsible may be liable in law accordingly.

Imprint:

Copyright © 2017 GRIN Verlag
Print and binding: Books on Demand GmbH, Norderstedt Germany
ISBN: 9783668632271

This book at GRIN:

https://www.grin.com/document/388434

Samiha Jiwan

The Canadian Residential School System and Cultural Genocide

GRIN Verlag

GRIN - Your knowledge has value

Since its foundation in 1998, GRIN has specialized in publishing academic texts by students, college teachers and other academics as e-book and printed book. The website www.grin.com is an ideal platform for presenting term papers, final papers, scientific essays, dissertations and specialist books.

Visit us on the internet:

http://www.grin.com/

http://www.facebook.com/grincom

http://www.twitter.com/grin_com

"Killing the Indian in the Child": The Canadian Residential School System and Cultural Genocide

Beginning in the 1870's, over one hundred fifty thousand First Nations, Metis and Inuit children were forcibly taken from their families and placed in Indian Residential schools. Funded by the Canadian government and Christian led, the system sought to "kill the Indian in the child," the last institution not closing until 1996. The forcible assimilation of aboriginal children through the residential school system greatly contributed to the cultural genocide of Canadian aboriginals by breaking the links to their culture and identity, consequently threatening their existence as a group. The schools also forcibly assimilated the children into the "white-Canadian culture." Further to this, the residential school employees inflicted physical harm on the students which left physical and emotional scars that prevented them from functioning in their communities in the long run. This essay employs the term 'cultural genocide' based on the definition provided by The Truth and Reconciliation Commission of Canada which states that, "Cultural genocide is the destruction of those structures and practices that allow the group to continue as a group. States that engage in cultural genocide set out to destroy the political and social institutions of the targeted group. Land is seized, and populations are forcibly transferred and their movement is restricted. Languages are banned. Spiritual leaders are persecuted, spiritual practices are forbidden, and objects of spiritual value are confiscated and destroyed. And, most significantly to the issue at hand, families are disrupted to prevent the transmission of cultural values and identity from one generation to the next." (Truth and Reconciliation Commission of Canada 1).

The government-appointed missionaries who were in charge of Canadian Indian Residential Schools perhaps had the most prominent role in the Christian-led campaigns to ban Aboriginal spiritual practices and therefore strip the students of their cultural identity. In 1947, a Roman Catholic official explained that because Canada was widely considered a Christian nation, he saw no reason as to why the residential schools "should foster aboriginal beliefs" such as the Potlatch and the Sun Dance (the "Thirst Dance")[1] which he considered "devil worship" (Fontaine 96). These dances were foreign to traditional Christian practices and in some cases, were perceived to outwardly opposed Christian beliefs. By banning these communal dances, the

---

[1] Potlatch ceremonies could be held to celebrate the passing of names, titles and responsibilities of one chief to the eldest heir, distribute wealth, establish rank, to mark the passing of a chief or the head of a house, and to celebrate weddings and births. The Sundance is an annual ceremony in honour of the sun and participants prove bravery by overcoming painful rituals (Gadacz).

residential schools prevented students from participating in the activities that held a central position in their cultural identity. Furthermore, by condemning these activities and labeling them as "devil worship," the residential schools villainized the students' beliefs and thus forced them to dissociate from their culture in order to avoid being shunned by society.

In addition to banning rituals, items of significance were also confiscated from the children which further contributed to the eradication of aboriginal cultural identity. An example of this was in the Kamloops school where objects of aboriginal importance were destroyed by the institute officials (Fontaine 63). By confiscating such items, residential schools deemed objects that have symbolic value to aboriginal cultural identity as unacceptable and worthless. Therefore by physically destroying these symbols the schools effectively destroyed the cultural identity they represented. These actions clearly point to the existence of a cultural genocide as quoting the TRC definition, "...objects of spiritual value are confiscated and destroyed." (Truth and Reconciliation Commission of Canada 1)

The residential schools also enforced a policy of language suppression in the early 1970s. This policy banned aboriginal languages and in turn forced students to speak solely English or French depending on the location of the school. In the eyes of the First Nation' people, knowing their native languages is a prerequisite to truly understanding and identifying with their ways of life (Regan 73). Language serves as a way to articulate cultural identity and can shape the way we think[2]. Therefore, the banning of aboriginal languages restricted the students ability to think in certain ways that were valuable to the understanding and expressing their cultural identity. Thus, the impact of residential schools silencing aboriginal languages can be seen as equivalent to silencing the identity through which they perceive themselves and their world. This policy of banning languages explicitly falls within the crimes that the TRC considers to constitute cultural genocide as earlier defined. By instead forcing students to speak English or French, residential schools perhaps had the power to encourage the values of white-canadian culture and thus assimilate students into a culture that they originally did not identify with. The role residential schools played in robbing children of their cultural identity can thus only be understood when coupled with the efforts to assimilate them into a very different understanding of 'Canadian society'.

---

[2] Many studies have shown this, one of them is the study performed by Lera Boroditsky at Stanford University (https://www.edge.org/conversation/lera_boroditsky-how-does-our-language-shape-the-way-we-think)

Residential schools replaced the aboriginal culture that they snatched from the students with a system of indoctrination that forcibly assimilated them into the "white-Canadian" culture. The Canadian government believed that the 'savage','barbaric' and therefore 'uncivilized' ways of the aboriginals must be terminated (from the Statement on Indian Policy, 1969) and that if every aboriginal person could be absorbed into the white-canadian lifestyle, the government would not have to provide reserves, make peace treaties with aboriginal communities, and grant them legal rights (Fontaine 96). The primary goal of the residential school system between the 1950s and 1960s was the transformation of students by means of cultural assimilation (Regan 135). This included physically transforming the appearance of students by cutting their long hair which often held spiritual significance and also using toxic chemicals to bleach their darker skin (Hensley). Schools learned to justify their genocidal actions all over the country by arguing that becoming like the white-Canadian population would allow aboriginals to participate in society and function later on in life. It was as if the aboriginals had reached a stage of helplessness and backwardness that could only be rectified by the 'white- Canadian' saviour. The residential schools expressed a paternalistic attitude towards the aboriginals such that assimilating them was an act of benevolence as opposed to a genocidal crime. Ironically, it is this very logic that justified expressing cultural intolerance.

Furthermore, students' aboriginal names were often replaced with Christian names in an effort to assimilate them into society. For example in 1847, at the Qu'Appelle residential school in Saskatchewan, a boy by the name of Ochankugahe was renamed David Kennedy, after the biblical character (Tait 42). In this way, he was subject to assimilation into the Christian culture that dominated Canada at the time. The Truth and Reconciliation Commission of Canada, a section of the Residential Schools Settlement Agreement that aims to inform all Canadians about what occurred in the residential school system, reveals a number of survivors who are struggling with re-claiming their aboriginal identity after being victims of residential schools. It includes a number of students whose aboriginal names were forcibly changed to Christian names or numbers (Regan 64). Names can be seen as the primary identifiers for human beings, and renaming the students with Christian names that hold no value or meaning for them robs them of their right to their own identity. It also forces them to take on an identity that does not reflect their own cultural experiences and thus compromises their individuality. Names often indicate what group an individual belongs to; they might convey to others what religious, ethnic or tribal group one belongs to. Therefore, the forced name replacements as a way of assimilating aboriginal students directly challenges the children's group affiliations. If names are understood as a loose type of structure that "allows group formation and continuation," the residential schools' efforts to change students' names was clearly a tool of cultural genocide as per the TRC definition (Truth and Reconciliation Commission of Canada) .

Lastly, the methods that residential schools used to both ban aboriginal practices and forcibly assimilate students into the dominating white culture were extremely brutal. As a result, the harm inflicted on the students in the residential school system left physical and emotional long-term effects on the children which presented many obstacles to their future participation in society. Students were conditioned to abandon their aboriginal identity and assimilate themselves through physical abuse. Punishments for displaying any aboriginal culture included beatings, food deprivation and public humiliation (Fontaine 123). For this reason, many aboriginal children today face abuse from their parents, many of whom were victims of residential schools and now suffer from drug and alcohol addictions (Tait 72). The acts of physical abuse used in the residential school system has negatively affected the former students ability to raise their own children and encouraged them to adopt the punishment methods they were exposed to in their youth.

A number of students also endured sexual abuse by schools' administration and impregnated students were often sent away for abortions to remote facilities such as the West Coast General Hospital. In 2006 Elaine Durocher Rather, a residential school survivor explains how this abuse led to loss of morals as she said, "...I could pull tricks as a prostitute, that's what the residential school taught me. It taught me how to lie, how to manipulate, how to exchange sexual favours for cash, meals, whatever, whatever the case may be" (qtd. In Hensley). The long term physical and mental effects of sexual abuse in residential schools trap victims in a cycle where their experiences largely influence the course of their future. More specifically, the systematic sexual abuse of children reinforces certain behaviours that they carry throughout their lives. As Rather's comment explains, children learn to use sexual activities as a means of survival instead of working towards obtaining an education and honourable employment. The abuse that children faced continue to stand as obstacles to leading arguably healthy and fulfilling lives in their adulthood.

To add to the horrors, the poor conditions and sanitation as well as inadequate food (sometimes even poison) resulted in sickness and death (Regan 25). Those who died of diseases such as tuberculosis were often sent back to their reserves to die or buried in the back of the school. If sickness did not claim a student's life, suicide often did. The system left scars on the students that discouraged continuing to live, thereby reflecting the existence of childhood depression which has ramifications for the children's future. The developing issues in regards with suicidal mind-sets throughout residential school survivors is a lasting consequence of genocidal crimes since mental illnesses such as depression continue to surface amongst former students (Fontaine 124).

Even when and if students were allowed to return home, they faced numerous struggles. The majority of them were unable to speak their mother tongue, thus restricting communication with their families (Regan 23). Many former students also found themselves unable to integrate within white-Canadian society nor return to their aboriginal culture. Struggling with the sense of belonging, the rippled effect of negative behaviours and communal degression disabled former students to build a healthy family. This inability to heal which is supported by the TRC definition of cultural genocide, when the disruption of families "to prevent the transmission of cultural values and identity from one generation to the next" is perhaps the most detrimental result of the abuse prevalent in the residential school system (Truth and Reconciliation Commission of Canada 1).

Many argue that the residential school system did not commit a cultural genocide and there are no legal implications because the term 'cultural genocide' is not used under international law. This is based off of the fact that the United Nations definition of genocide does not address "cultural genocide". However, the same United Nations definition does state that, "a genocide may include mental harm to a racial or religious group…" which undoubtedly occurred via the residential school system as proven thoroughly in the previous arguments. (United Nations Convention on the Prevention and Punishment of the crime of genocide 3).

In conclusion, the Residential School system destroyed the lives of many aboriginal children all across the country. The schools forbade the spiritual and cultural rituals of the aboriginal children and therefore stole their cultural identity and contributed to the destruction of their traditions. Furthermore, residential schools forcibly assimilate aboriginal children into the "white-Canadian" culture resulting in the adoption of an artificial identity. Lastly, the physical and emotional scars left by the school system, prevented and continues to prevent the victims from functioning in their communities. As stated in the TRC definition of a cultural genocide, these long term effects can perhaps be seen as the most traumatic and most significant issue, as "families are disrupted to prevent the transmission of cultural values and identity from one generation to the next " (Truth and Reconciliation Commission of Canada).

The Indian Residential school issue is undoubtedly a dark chapter of Canadian history, and the repercussions of the horrific actions leave many still searching for closure. The schools played a significant role in the cultural genocide of Canadian aboriginals by severing the links to their cultural identity which in turn, threatened their existence as a group. Looking forward, recognizing the activities of the residential schools as genocidal crimes raises several important questions about reconciliation, responsibility and accountability. As Canadians, these are questions that we must try to answer as they are essential to fostering a society that is accepting and appreciative of the cultural diversity that colours our collective history.

References

Boroditsky, Lera. "How Does Our Language Shape the Way we Think?." *Edge*. Edge Foundation Inc, 6 Nov. 2009. Web. 17 Aug 2017. <https://www.edge.org/conversation/lera_boroditsky-how-does-our-language-shape-the-way-we-think>.

Fontaine, Phil. *A Knock on the Door*. Winnipeg: University of Manitoba Press, 2016. Print.

Gadacz, Rene. "Sun Dance." *The Canadian Encyclopedia*. 2006. Historica Canada. Web 17 Aug. 2017.<http://www.thecanadianencyclopedia.ca/en/article/sun-dance/>.

Hensley, Laura. "Residential School System was 'Cultural Genocide.'" *National Post Online*. National Post, 9 July 2015. Web. 17 Aug. 2017. <http://news.nationalpost.com/tag/cultural-genocide>.

Regan, Paulette. *Unsettling the Settler Within*. Vancouver: University of British Columbia Press, 2010. Print.

Tait, Caroline. "Fetal Alcohol Syndrome Among Aboriginal People in Canada: Review and Analysis of the Intergenerational Links to Residential Schools." *The Aboriginal Healing Foundation*. Cultural and Mental Health Research Unit., 2003. Web. 17 Aug 2017. <http://www.ahf.ca/downloads/fetal-alcohol-syndrome.pdf>.

Truth and Reconciliation Committee of Canada. "Executive Summary: Honouring the Truth, Reconciling for the Future." (n.p.), July 23, 2015. Web. 17 Aug 2017.
<http://www.trc.ca/websites/trcinstitution/File/2015/Honouring_the_Truth_Reconciling_for_the_Future_July_23_2015.pdf>.

United Nations. "Office of the UN Special Adviser On The Prevention Of Genocide." (n.p.), Sep 12, 2016. Web. 17 Aug 2017. http://www.un.org/en/preventgenocide/adviser/pdf/osapg_analysis_framework.pdf

YOUR KNOWLEDGE HAS VALUE

- We will publish your bachelor's and master's thesis, essays and papers

- Your own eBook and book - sold worldwide in all relevant shops

- Earn money with each sale

Upload your text at www.GRIN.com
and publish for free